Original title:
Space-Time Shenanigans

Copyright © 2025 Creative Arts Management OÜ
All rights reserved.

Author: Derek Caldwell
ISBN HARDBACK: 978-1-80567-817-5
ISBN PAPERBACK: 978-1-80567-938-7

A Chaotic Constellation

Stars collide in a silly dance,
Bright comets giggle, given a chance.
Planets spin with a wobbly grace,
While black holes play hide and seek in space.

Floating socks in the cosmic swirl,
Astronauts tumble, giving a twirl.
Galaxies burst into popcorn pops,
As spacetime folds, and laughter never stops.

The Riddle of Reality

Time drips like honey from a sweet jar,
Ticking clocks cheekily tease from afar.
Wormholes giggle, 'Come take a peek!'
Twists and turns make the cosmos squeak.

Quantum cats lounge in lazy moods,
Dodging questions, befriending feuds.
Folded moments, a comical sight,
Chasing each other like kids in the night.

Cosmic Ripples

Ripples in space like a water slide,
Planets splash as they take the ride.
Neutron stars strut in sequined gowns,
Wobbling wildly while spacetime frowns.

Black holes snicker at gravity's grasp,
Fuzzy edges in a light-speed gasp.
Quasars blink with a cheeky grin,
Silly shadows where the fun begins.

Laughing Through Lightyears

Zooming past stars in a brightly lit car,
Giggles echo from near and far.
Lightyears stretch like a rubber band,
Time travelers chuckle, it's oh-so-grand.

Shooting stars dash with playful glee,
Making wishes on cosmic tea.
Voyagers dance through dimension's play,
Seeking joy in the interstellar way.

When Stars Collide with Yesterday

In the sky, a star fell down,
Danced with time, wore a crown.
Yesterday laughed, tripped on a shoe,
Said, "I'm late, what about you?"

Galaxies giggled, spun in delight,
Caught in a waltz, a comical sight.
Jupiter winked, said with a grin,
"Why's everyone late? Did we forget to begin?"

The Interstellar Clockmaker

A clockmaker spun gears made of stars,
Wound up the cosmos, played with Mars.
"Oops!" he said, as time slipped away,
"Guess I'll just fix it another day!"

He added some glitter, a sprinkle of beams,
"Don't worry, it's fine!" he said with his dreams.
When asked what was wrong, he twinkled his eye,
"Time's just a concept, like pie in the sky!"

Cosmic Capers Among the Planets

Venus and Pluto played tag in the night,
While Saturn spun rings—what a delightful sight!
Neptune brought snacks, in waves full of zest,
"Grab a comet, it's better than a fest!"

Earth offered jokes, warped under the sun,
Laughter like stardust, oh what fun!
Eclipses were chuckles, Moon rolled with glee,
As the stars danced along, carefree as can be.

Whispers of the Quantum Realms

In tiny dimensions, giggles abound,
Particles waltz without making a sound.
"Are you here? Or are you not?"
The quarks just winked, what a funny plot!

A photon declared, "I'm both here and there,
I travel so fast, just don't need a fare!"
The universe chuckled, in waves of delight,
As they murmured secrets late into the night.

The Gravity Between Us

You pulled me close, like a comet's tail,
In this dance of stars, we'll never fail.
I tripped on moonbeams while reaching for you,
Our laughter echoed in a cosmic hue.

We wobbled through orbits, giddy with glee,
Like planets colliding, just you and me.
With each little twist, we spun round and round,
Creating a whirlpool of joy that we found.

Currents of the Celestial Sea

Oh, sailing the cosmos, what a bright show,
In a paper boat made of stardust and glow.
The waves of the vacuum tickle our feet,
With jellyfish planets, oh, what a treat!

We surf on the light beams, riding the tide,
With an octopus captain, our joys multiplied.
A splash in the dark void, we giggle and cheer,
While aliens chuckle and hug us so near.

Nebulae of Nostalgia

In the clouds of the past, we float like two kids,
Wiggling through memories, flipping our lids.
With candy floss planets, oh, sweet and bright,
We reminisce laughter that sparkled like light.

The echoes of moments, like shooting stars flash,
While we munch on dreams with a whimsical bash.
In this colorful haze, we smile and we sigh,
Finding joy in the hours that zip by and fly.

Temporal Travelers' Tales

With a wink and a nod, we jump through the clocks,
Sharing silly stories as time softly rocks.
In pajamas of starlight, we giggle and spin,
Each second's a riddle, let the fun begin!

We visit the past, just to swipe some old snacks,
While future us wave from their shiny hedgebacks.
With each flip of a hourglass, all bets are off,
We belly laugh hard, can't help but scoff!

The Timekeeper's Trick

In a clock shop strange and quirky,
The hands danced fast and sometimes jerky.
Each tick a giggle, each tock a cheer,
Lost a whole week or just a mere year.

With gears that wink and springs that tease,
Time hops around like it's got the keys.
Tickle the seconds, flip through the past,
In this wild ride, moments fly fast.

Paradoxical Pathways

Two roads diverged in a cosmic maze,
One leads to laughter, the other to haze.
Take a left for giggles, a right for a scream,
Wander too long, and you'll unravel the dream.

With every turn, logic takes a break,
A jester jumps out, just for laughs' sake.
A loop-de-loop round space and time,
Brought forth a cat in a top hat mime.

Gravity's Playful Prank

Once gravity fled on a sunny day,
Floated the world in a whimsical sway.
From topsy to turvy, all danced in the air,
A cow on a star laughed without a care.

With giggles that echoed like cosmic clowns,
Buildings did somersaults, upside-down towns.
Then gravity chuckled and said, 'I'm back!'
And down came the giggles with a wonderful whack!

When Stars Collide

Two stars met over a cup of bright tea,
Bumping and swirling, 'Oh, pardon me!'
They laughed as they struggled to find their own light,
Creating a spectacle, a cosmic delight.

With a wink and a twist, they tumbled in dance,
Forming a comet, a glittering chance.
When night fell, they shined, dazzling and wide,
A sparkly show of how dreams collide.

The Tick-Tock Troupe

In a clock that spins like a top,
Dancers leap and never stop.
Each tick-tock a quirky beat,
They tangle up their dancing feet.

With a wink, they twist time's flow,
Making hours melt like snow.
They giggle at the past and present,
Turning minutes into a sentiment.

Comet Chasing Curiosities

Comets zoom with tails so bright,
Chasing wonders in the night.
Aliens wave from every stream,
Brewing mischief, like a dream.

They race against the moon's sly grin,
Daring each other to begin.
Asteroids chuckle in their paths,
As comets dance, they share their laughs.

Wibbly-Wobbly Dimensions

In a realm where rules bend and sway,
Reality takes a holiday,
With a bounce, a twist, and a turn,
Wibbly-wobbly, we laugh and learn.

Here, gravity plays peek-a-boo,
And time can dance a jig or two.
We ride the fun on a squishy plane,
Finding joy in the absurdity's gain.

Loops of Light

Zipping through the loops so bright,
Laser beams and laughter ignite.
Hopping through colors, oh what a sight,
Silly shadows dance with delight.

In spirals that spin like a top,
We lose ourselves and never stop.
Each loop a chance for a giggle spree,
In a carnival of light, wild and free.

Whims of the Universe

In a realm where clocks tick backwards,
Cats might dance with sparkling stars.
Planets wear their silliest hats,
While jellybeans float in jars.

Gravity's a prankster, you see,
It loves to let you fly for fun.
A trampoline made of candy dreams,
Bouncing past the morning sun.

One day it rains a rainbow's spark,
And cupcakes grow from trees of light.
Time giggles like a mischievous child,
As night turns into silly bright.

So join the games of cosmic cheer,
Where laughter stretches through the air.
The universe winks, its secrets clear,
In this playful, whimsical affair.

The Multiversal Masquerade

In galaxies where jesters gleam,
And penguins waddle curiously,
Everyone wears a fishy dream,
    At the ball of absurdity.

A unicorn sips lemonade,
While frogs recite poetic rhymes.
The clocks all melt, they're unafraid,
As laughter dances through the chimes.

Nebulae spin in joyful tizz,
Juggling moons with a comical flair.
In this dance, there's nothing amiss,
    Just delight swirling everywhere.

So grab your mask, let's twirl around,
    With stars as our funky guides.
In a masquerade, joy is found,
Where the whimsical always resides.

Fractured Moments

Wibbly wobbly clocks go tick,
While turtles bask in cosmic rays.
A sandwich slips, it's quite a trick,
As time takes funny, wild delays.

In a split second, leaps abound,
Bananas wear their helmets right.
The past and future spin around,
In this odd, delightful flight.

Each time you blink, a cat's a dog,
And dogs just dance in silly suits.
Reality's a playful fog,
Filled with confetti and strange hoots.

So ponder not the flipped-up views,
But savor each bizarre twist.
In fractured moments, there's a muse,
Of whimsical wonders to enlist.

Astral Antics

Stars play tag in midnight's chill,
While asteroids do the hula hoop.
Galaxies giggle, what a thrill,
As comets lead the goofy troop.

Planets roll like marbles bright,
Jokes echo through the vast expanse.
Dancing on the edge of light,
Chaos joins in the cosmic dance.

With each twinkle, a laugh is found,
As stardust scatters all around.
The universe jests, no reason bound,
In wacky sights, true joy is crowned.

So lift your gaze to skies above,
And join the frolic, let dreams soar.
In astral antics, spiced with love,
Adventure's waiting at the core.

Echoes of Distant Moments

I found my socks in 2049,
A tangled mess with a slice of lime.
They danced about like tiny freaks,
While I just stared in disbelief for weeks.

A cat in space began to meow,
Chasing moonbeams, I don't know how.
It slipped through time, a cosmic slide,
While I just waited, arms open wide.

My coffee brewed in a different year,
With sprinkles of stardust, oh so near.
I took a sip and started to float,
Floating back to my old life, what a joke!

In a bubble of giggles, I chase my fate,
Wobbling on a timeline that's hard to sate.
But each twist and turn feels so right,
Laughing with echoes that light up the night.

Gravity's Playful Tricks

I tripped over a star on my way to work,
It winked and laughed, oh what a jerk!
My sandwich flew to the fifth dimension,
Into a realm of spurious invention.

Down came my hat, doing the twist,
Defying gravity, oh, what a tryst!
As I chased it through interstellar paths,
I couldn't help but giggle at its gaffes.

A jellybean floated with such grace,
Caught in a loop of a time-bird's chase.
It taunted me from a quirky place,
A sweet little jest in this cosmic race.

Laughing as I navigated this bizarre spree,
I realized life's a grand cosmic tea.
Where gravity plays, and tricks abound,
I danced with joy on this merry ground.

A Symphony of Cosmic Echoes

In the orchestra of stars, I found my tune,
The bass was a giant, bouncing like a moon.
The violins wobbled in a comical spree,
As I joined the chaos, feeling so free.

A comet flew by with a sly little grin,
Playing the horn while I couldn't help in.
The echoes laughed in a cosmic giggle,
As I tried to dance but ended up in a wiggle.

The flutes sparkled and glimmered like light,
As I hummed along in sheer delight.
With each note bending the fabric of space,
I lost my shoes in this cosmic grace.

The audience of planets cheered with a clap,
While I stumbled around, not quite in my nap.
Yet every quirk made the concert divine,
A symphony of laughter, perfectly out of line.

Wandering Through Dimensions

I took a step into a door ajar,
And landed in a land where cows drive cars.
They mooed with style, wearing shades of blue,
While I just laughed, not knowing what to do.

A time-traveling frog hopped by my side,
Telling me tales of a whimsical ride.
We jumped through portals with quite a flair,
Each leap a riddle in the sweet, cool air.

In a realm where clouds made of candy floss,
I lost my hat; oh, what a toss!
The trees taught me how to do the cha-cha,
As I twirled around like a confused llama.

Wandering here, it's all a delight,
Time and direction just don't feel right.
With each new twist, I grin with glee,
In this silly land, I'm forever free.

Fractured Moments in Orbital Dreams

In a galaxy not far away,
A cow danced the night away.
Stars burst forth in a playful twirl,
As comets lag behind, in a whirl.

A clock sang songs of silly time,
Each tick a rhyme, each tock a chime.
Wormholes giggled as they spun,
While planets played tag just for fun.

Meteor showers rained jellybeans,
Aliens snacked on candy machines.
Gravity took a holiday,
As moons pranced around in a ballet.

In this chaos, a paradox spun,
Where yesterday's work was just begun.
So, if you trip on beams of light,
Just laugh, my friend, it's all alright!

A Cosmic Riddle in Infinite Loops

A riddle echoed, loud and clear,
Why do asteroids disappear?
Every spin they make, they tease,
Those roundabouts bring cosmic sneeze!

Planets lined up for a parade,
Saturn lost its ring; quite the trade!
Venus slipped on a banana peel,
The sun just chuckled, 'What a meal!'

Time keeps playing peek-a-boo,
A game of hide and seek for two.
Every second hides a surprise,
With giggles hidden in the skies.

So grab your hat, let's zoom and glide,
Through quirky realms, we'll take a ride.
Forget the rules, let's take a chance,
In this wild, cosmic, wacky dance!

Time's Glimmering Mirage

A mirage shimmered on the ground,
With clocks that laughed and silly sounds.
Days grew longer, then took naps,
As seconds danced in crazy laps.

Tick tock tangoed with a breeze,
Ticklish years brought us to our knees.
Moments floated in fluffy balls,
As time slipped through, it had no walls.

Watch the past give future a wink,
As shadows sip on lemonade pink.
The calendar juggled its weeks,
While history giggled and sneezed.

Join the fun, don't hesitate,
As echoes bounce through the cosmic gate.
In this mirage of laughter and light,
Take a leap; it feels just right!

Unraveling Temporal Threads

With threads of time in tangled knots,
A cat chased yarn in the cosmic spots.
Each pull revealed a brand new scene,
Where hiccuping stars burst in between.

Ticklish clocks tried to unwind,
Chasing moments they'd left behind.
Through fabric woven from giggles and glee,
In this quilted chaos, we roam free.

Einstein shared a joke with the moon,
While gravity hummed a jolly tune.
As past and future did a flip,
We sailed on this cosmic trip.

So let's embrace the silly swirl,
Where every quirk makes our heads twirl.
In unraveling threads, laughter ignites,
In this dance of time, we take flight!

The Jovian Jester's Journey

In the land of swirling storms,
A jester danced on whirling forms.
With giggles twinkling in his eyes,
He whispered jokes to thunderous skies.

He rode on clouds of whipped-up cream,
With Saturn's rings, he'd often scheme.
A yo-yo flight around the sun,
His laughter echoed, oh so fun!

Meteors caught in his playful sway,
Twirling like children at play.
While asteroids grinned, they'd cheer and sing,
As he juggled comet tails, a cosmic fling!

So gather round and give a cheer,
For the jester's antics far and near.
In the realm where gravity bends,
He'll keep us laughing till the end!

Lullabies of Lightyears

Shooting stars across the sky,
A lullaby from worlds gone by.
Each twinkle holds a silly tale,
Of alien cats on moons that sail.

Galaxies wink with goofy glee,
Singing to you, come hop with me!
In wormholes where the giggles roam,
The universe feels just like home.

Traveling through a cosmic maze,
We'll dance and sing through nebula haze.
Time's a prankster, oh what a tease,
As we float on cosmic breezes with ease.

So cuddle up in starlit dreams,
Where every joke's stitched with moonbeams.
In the melody of the vast unknown,
Let laughter guide you, you're not alone!

Trysts with the Temperamental Universe

Stars and planets played hide and seek,
With comets teasing, oh so cheek.
The universe chuckled, a fickle friend,
Turning serious fun 'til the very end.

Black holes with secrets big and bold,
Holding mysteries that never grow old.
Yet with a wink, they start to sway,
As gravity pulls our cares away.

Quasars blink in a cosmic jest,
Waving at us from their stellar nest.
Time loops laugh at every fumble,
As we dance through stardust, take a tumble!

With a wink and a smile, it's clear to see,
The universe sets our spirits free.
In the midst of chaos and cosmic schemes,
Find joy in the oddness, chase your dreams!

Merrymaking among Moons

Underneath a dancing moon,
Jovial spirits start to croon.
Swinging through the Milky Way,
They tease the night, come out and play.

With each glimmer, laughter spills,
Echoes ripple through cosmic hills.
Galactic games with friends in tow,
Chasing shadows, hiding from woe.

Moons with faces, smiling bright,
Join the party, what a sight!
As meteors race and comets glide,
We celebrate galactic pride.

So raise a glass to the stellar spree,
Where joy's the compass, wild and free.
In this universe where humor blooms,
Let's dance forever among the moons!

Chrono-Chasms

A clock that laughs, with hands that play,
It ticks in odd, peculiar ways.
Time jumps and skips, a silly dance,
As I fall into a temporal chance.

In a pudding pie, I found a date,
Spoonfuls of laughter, oh, how great!
Muffins whisper secrets of the past,
As I munch on memories, made to last.

A bouncy ball that rolls through ages,
Collects the humor of ancient sages.
The jester's cap spins through the day,
While futures giggle and farce in play.

With a wink from stars, I chase and chase,
A chase with giggles, a cosmic race.
I slip through wormholes, like a playful breeze,
In this funny realm, I laugh with ease.

Jests of the Infinite Canvas

A brush that paints with silly strokes,
Colors leap and giggle in pokes.
The sun wears shades, the moon makes jokes,
As clouds drift by, and laughter chokes.

A canvas stretches, twists, and bends,
Creating paths where giggle never ends.
The stars have hats, the comets laugh loud,
As I swim in humor, oh, feeling proud!

Each planet spins with a goofy face,
While meteors dance in a cosmic race.
In this gallery of the bizarre,
Even the black holes have rhythm, ajar.

A rainbow slides with a giddy cheer,
Every color whispers, "Come near, come here!"
Together we frolic, with no time to waste,
In this gallery of giggles, oh, what a taste!

Galaxies of Giggles

Where stardust swirls like cotton candy,
Laughter bounces, sweet and dandy.
Celestial clowns in a dizzy whirl,
Each twinkling star gives a comical twirl.

Comets zoom with a chuckle and glide,
While black holes beckon with humor inside.
Planets play tag, round and round,
In the cosmic circus, giggles abound.

A joke from Mars makes Jupiter grin,
As they dance in orbits, chubby and thin.
Meteor showers with puns in their flight,
Light up the night with laughter so bright.

Through galaxies spinning in riotous beams,
I savor the humor, and chase my dreams.
Each chuckle a star in the infinite sky,
In this universe of joy, I zoom by.

The Hilarious Hyperspace

I zipped through folds of fabric and time,
In a super silly, galactic grime.
The speed of giggles, a warp factor fun,
Where every joke is a dazzling run.

A wormhole hiccup, oh what a sight,
It burps out laughs, and tickles the night.
With every loop, I roll on the floor,
While the stars snicker and beg for more.

Hyperspace hopping, I laugh so hard,
As I play hide and seek with a shiny star.
They peek and they giggle, a luminous clan,
In this madcap journey, all part of the plan.

So strap in tight for this goofy ride,
As we race with mirth through the universe wide.
With every twist and cosmic pitch,
Perspective is key, to giggle and switch.

Orbiting the Echo of Time

In a rocket made of cheese,
With a cat that loves to sneeze,
We twirl and whirl around the sun,
Counting laughs, oh what fun!

A clock that dances on its hands,
Sipping tea on distant sands,
It giggles as the hours fly,
While we just wave, ask and sigh.

Planets play a game of tag,
While comets dance and stars all brag,
We ride the wind like feathered kites,
Sailing through the cosmic lights.

So hold your breath, let's take a chance,
In this universe of silly dance,
With echoes ringing all around,
Together, joy is always found.

The Moon's Lament for Lost Hours

Oh Moon, you glow with wistful glee,
But don't you worry about me,
I lost my socks in time's wide void,
Now they float, both lost and buoyed.

With every quarter, I feel so grand,
Yet tripping on craters wasn't planned,
You shine so bright, yet I still frown,
Where'd that hourglass go, oh brown?

The stars they giggle, the nebulae tease,
As I trip over light, a cosmic breeze,
I laugh aloud through cosmic strife,
Wondering where I parked my life.

So pull me close, oh lunar friend,
Let's dance until the cosmos ends,
I'll write a poem, just for you,
A funny tale, our time to skew.

Fractal Dreams in Celestial Gardens

In gardens where the fractals bloom,
I hiccup jokes that chase the gloom,
With flowers painted in silly hues,
They giggle softly as I muse.

Each petal spins a tale so bright,
Of singing stars that dance at night,
We bounce on beams like silly sprites,
In dreams with fractals, oh what sights!

A sandwich made of stardust treat,
Makes me laugh while on my feet,
Gravity's grip may try to bind,
But silliness is what I find.

So drink the nectar, rich and sweet,
In gardens where the dreams entreat,
With laughter echoing through the air,
These zany realms are beyond compare.

Chasing Light, Forgetting Time

I sprint ahead where shadows play,
Chasing light, so bright and gay,
But as I run, I trip and fall,
Forgetting what I had to call.

The sun winks twice, a cheeky tease,
As I chase it, giggling with ease,
Time is a prankster, slipping sly,
With every step, it waves goodbye.

Through sparkles and beams I wildly glide,
As moments scatter, I laugh with pride,
Here's a joke, a pun, a rhyme,
In this madness, I lose my time.

So come with me on this wild race,
Through realms of light, we'll find our place,
With every chuckle, we'll ignite,
A world where joy is pure delight.

Starlit Whispers of Tomorrow

Stars giggle as they twirl,
Planets tease in a cosmic swirl.
Time slips by on a comet's tail,
We chase it down, but it's always pale.

Galaxies wink with a cheeky grace,
Twirling spaceships in a race.
Black holes laugh with a hearty cheer,
'Come get lost! We've got no fear!'

Wormholes bend with a silly twist,
'Join us! You can't resist!'
Rockets zoom with a whoop and shout,
Exploring the quirks of the cosmic rout.

So grab a star and hold it tight,
Let's disappear into the night.
In the laughter of the universe wide,
We'll float together, our joy the guide.

Echoes from Distant Horizons

Echoes travel on a laser beam,
Tickling thoughts like a funny dream.
Quantum giggles in the air,
Spinning tales beyond compare.

From the moons of Mars comes a chuckle,
While Venus plays with a cosmic trickle.
Pulsars dance, flashing bright,
Sending jokes through the endless night.

Novae pop like confetti bright,
Celebrating with all their might.
Time loops in a playful jest,
Encouraging us to take a rest.

Through the orbits, laughter blooms,
In the darkness, joy consumes.
With echoes guiding our silly way,
We'll explore forever and a day.

A Dance with the Cosmic Clock

The clock ticks slow, then speeds in a whirl,
Hours giggle, as they zoom and twirl.
'Step right up! Don't be late!'
Time's a clown with a playful fate.

Seconds boogie, minutes jive,
Caught in a dance where all's alive.
With each step, laughter grows,
Riding the rhythm where no one knows.

Planets shimmy, stars will dip,
Together we take a wild trip.
Tick and tock spin round the floor,
Grinning as we ask for more.

With every turn, a giggle escapes,
In this ballroom of cosmic shapes.
So grab your partner, give a shock,
Join in the dance with the cosmic clock!

Nebulae and Nonsense

In a cloud of colors, jokes collide,
Nebulae whirl in a rainbow ride.
Asteroids chuckle, comets hiss,
Creating a cosmic, funny bliss.

Stars throw bubbles, each one a tale,
Galaxies skate on a cosmic rail.
Light years tease, whispering 'Hey!',
'Come join our nonsense, come play!'

Quasars flicker, winking bright,
They share secrets of the night.
With every twirl, they chuckle along,
In the universe's grand, silly song.

So join the fun, let laughter fly,
With nebulae and nonsense up high.
In this frolic of cosmic glee,
We'll find joy in infinity!

The Time Weaver's Folly

A clock ticked back, a cat meowed,
The past and future both disallowed.
I slipped on time, a slippery slope,
Lost in a world of cosmic antelope.

The weaver laughed, a stitch gone awry,
I chased a comet, oh my, oh my!
Through wormholes wild, I tumbled and spun,
What fun to be lost when you're never done.

A donut-shaped planet, a jellybean sun,
I danced with a robot, all in good fun.
With each twist and turn, my luck seemed to sway,
But what's time to a jester? Let's play all day!

So here I remain, a mischievous sprite,
Juggling the cosmos from day into night.
A patchwork of moments, a tapestry grand,
The folly of weaving was simply unplanned!

Galactic Gaffes

An asteroid belt, a bumper car's fate,
I zigged when I should have zagged, oh mate!
With meteors flying like confetti in space,
I tripped on a beam and fell flat on my face.

In a nebula bright, I lost my way,
A dancing star whispered, 'Come out and play!'
I twirled with a quasar, got dizzy and spun,
In galactic chaos, I stumbled for fun.

A UFO buzzed, with aliens all grins,
They offered me snacks with gummy bear fins.
I cracked a joke, they laughed 'til they cried,
In this universe, we share a wild ride.

So let's toast to blunders, to laughs shared in flight,
In the cosmic carnival, everything feels right.
With slip-ups and laughter, we'll never grow old,
In the universe's book, our stories are told!

The Mischief of Moments

In a blink, I was here, then there, then not,
Time played a trick, a puzzling plot.
I spilled my tea in a time-warped dance,
And hopped through a doorway, given the chance.

With seconds like gumdrops, sweet and absurd,
Each moment a hiccup, a whimsical word.
I made a new friend, a time-traveling snail,
We plotted our travels on a banana peel trail.

Together we plotted, a caper so bold,
Playing hopscotch on stardust, the future untold.
A mischief of moments, that's how it seemed,
In the clockwork of mischief, we endlessly dreamed.

So here's to the chaos, the fun we will keep,
In this zany adventure, we never lose sleep.
In the scrapbook of life, let's jot down the sites,
Of moments so silly, they burst into lights!

Pulsars and Puzzles

A pulsar beamed bright, with a wink and a grin,
It played hide and seek with the stars deep within.
I solved cosmic riddles, each twist a delight,
As galaxies giggled in the velvety night.

I found a black hole named Benny, a tease,
It swallowed my sandwich, I fell to my knees!
With laughter exploding like supernova fires,
I sang to the cosmos, fulfilling my desires.

Jumbling my timelines, a quantum ballet,
I skipped with the particles, what a fine day!
With spinning equations and riddles so round,
In the whirl of the cosmos, pure joy can be found.

So twirl with a neutron, embrace every jest,
In the puzzles of stardust, we're all truly blessed.
For every odd chuckle, each twist we pursue,
Is a reminder the universe giggles with you!

The Cosmic Carousel

Round and round we seem to spin,
The stars all laugh as we begin.
Mars took a ride, then fell off quick,
Jupiter's clowning made us all sick.

Saturn's rings are a circus cape,
With aliens dancing, a cosmic shape.
We're dizzy now, what a wild place,
In this merry-go-round of outer space.

Celestial Disarray

Planets bump in a cosmic race,
Comets wearing silly face.
Uranus giggles, it can't be serious,
As black holes try to act most curious.

Neptune tripped over a shooting star,
While Venus sings from her solar car.
Galactic pranks make us spin and sway,
In this jumbled, joyful, starry play.

Time-Traveling Trivialities

A dapper dinosaur from long ago,
Wore a top hat with a bow.
He stepped in time, what a sight to see,
Now he's late for tea, oh dear me!

Future folks with their silly dreams,
Juggling time like it's made of beams.
They clown around, just like jesters,
Bending hours like fun-filled jesters.

Singularity Shenanigans

A wormhole tricks a daring crew,
Into a selfie with a kangaroo.
Laughter echoes through the dark,
As time loops start to leave a mark.

Zany twists that make one grin,
As they forgot where they've been.
A bouncing light, a giggling cheer,
In this wild ride, not a single fear.

Celestial Whirlwinds

In a galaxy where cows can fly,
Planets dance and wink their eye.
A comet's tail, a wagging tongue,
In cosmic jokes, the stars are hung.

Moonbeams chase the milky way,
While Martians sing, 'Let's have a play!'
Asteroids grin as they roll around,
In this swirling mess, laughter is found.

Galactic winds toss comets in fits,
As black holes giggle in bottomless pits.
With meteors throwing confetti bright,
The universe chuckles all through the night.

So let's twirl through the cosmic breeze,
With humor born from stars and trees.
A joyful romp in the vast expanse,
Where every quasar joins the dance.

Chrono Dances in the Void

Time skips like a child at play,
Bouncing back to yesterday.
Tick-tock, the clock is wrong,
In this wibbly-wobbly gong.

A jesting hourglass spills its sand,
Past and future, hand in hand.
When seconds trip on their own feet,
Every moment's a silly treat.

Chronicles whirl in dizzying twirl,
As seconds give time a playful whirl.
Winking seconds spin and glide,
In this whimsical, wild ride.

So grab your shoes, let's start to spin,
In laughter, let the fun begin.
Through tangled knots of time we roam,
In ticklish realms we call our home.

The Timekeeper's Tumble

A timekeeper dropped his pocket watch,
It rolled and bounced with quite a swatch.
In its wake, hours skipped and danced,
While minutes twirled in a merry prance.

With every tick, time turned on its head,
As birthdays popped up, then fled.
Tomorrow's woes turned to yesterday's cheer,
In this playful mess, we found no fear.

Time juggles with a laughter clear,
As hours chase their own rear.
Poking fun at clocks on the wall,
In this tumble, we all have a ball.

So here's to the keeper, lost and found,
Whirling through moments, round and round.
In the circus of time, we twirl and sway,
With every stumble, we laugh and play.

Starlit Paradoxes

In a twinkling world of baffling light,
Stars tumble down, oh what a sight!
Aliens laugh in riddles profound,
As paradoxes spin round and round.

Time-folds create a comic spree,
Where yesterday's child plays with glee.
Future selves wave from the past,
In this quirky cosmos, fun is vast.

Galaxies hiccup in dizzy delight,
Chasing shadows into the night.
Light-years shuffle on feet of foam,
Making each cosmic wanderer feel at home.

So grab your broom and join the ride,
In the loops and bends, there's nothing to hide.
With laughter as our guiding star,
We'll dance through the oddness, near and far.

Astral Journeys Beyond the Now

A cat in a rocket, off with a meow,
Chasing a comet with a curious brow.
Socks from the future, they dance in the light,
Tickling the stars on a chilly night.

The moon's wearing glasses, quite high on a hill,
While planets play poker, with Martians for thrills.
Time does a jig as we skip in the air,
Laughing at logic, we float without care.

Frogs in the cosmos, they hop with a grin,
Dragging their friends from the depths of a bin.
Galactic confetti, it rains from above,
Each wink of a star shows the universe's love.

So grab your space boots, let's dance in a whirl,
With giggles and gaffes, round the quasar swirl.
Every odd minute, we turn and we leap,
In this cosmic circus, there's laughter to keep.

Celestial Whirlwinds

A whirlwind of colors spins round and 'round,
Kites made of stardust dance high off the ground.
Comets are laughing, some rolling in glee,
As galaxies juggle their solar debris.

Mars wears a halo, quite proud of its style,
While Jupiter winks, doing a jokester's smile.
Neptune is teasing, just pulling a prank,
As aliens laugh, floating high in their tank.

The sun tells a joke, then bursts into rays,
While Saturn joins in with its ring's sassy plays.
Time looping like hula hoops, round and around,
In this funny universe, silliness is found.

So let's swirl and twirl, leap from star to star,
Finding joy in the cosmos, wherever we are.
In a dance with the planets, we giggle and sway,
In the grand cosmic party, come join the ballet!

Chrono-Quest Adventures

A time-traveling toaster, it pops up with glee,
Toasting up bagels from 2033.
Caffeine from centuries past fills the air,
As knights try to surf on a time-bending chair.

Dinosaurs texting in dinosaur tongues,
While Shakespeare's sonnets sound all out of fun.
Wizards on hoverboards, zoom across time,
Crafting up potions that smell just like lime.

The future wears flip-flops, the past wears a crown,
In a quest through the ages, we bounce up and down.
Each tick of the clock holds a mystery bright,
We laugh with the seconds, it feels so delight!

So let's run with the minutes, play hopscotch with fate,
Riding through epochs, it's never too late.
Adventure awaits in the humor of now,
With giggles and cheers, we make our own vow!

The Temporal Tangle

In a tangle of timelines, a squirrel wears a hat,
Chasing his shadow, a little chitchat.
Yesterday's breakfast is rolling down hills,
While future's spaghetti just gives us the chills.

The watch on my wrist does a jig and a dance,
As candy from yesterday jumps at the chance.
We tickle the seconds, they giggle and squirm,
In this silly dimension, nothing's too firm.

A paradox leaps from the fridge with a pout,
While time marches forward and does a spin out.
With clocks upside down and calendars bent,
We share in the laughter, it's money well spent.

So let's twirl in the chaos, let's ride on the breeze,
With jesters and pixies, we do as we please.
In a tangle of time, we twinkle and twirl,
Eternally giggling in this wacky whirl!

Wandering within Whirlpools

In a swirl of socks and a shoe,
I tripped on the swirl of the blue.
The whirlpool giggled, took me for a spin,
Now I'm lost in a sock where the fun begins.

I met a cat with a hat in a dance,
He twirled and spun, giving me a chance.
With a blink, I'm in a place full of cheese,
Dancing with mice, oh, my laugh's sure to freeze!

The clocks are melting, time takes a snack,
While I leap through puddles in a funky track.
A jellyfish plays the ukulele crisp,
And the stars join in with a shimmering lisp.

As I whirl away on this silly spree,
I wave goodbye, cheese and mice sing to me.
In a bubbly laugh, I find the way back,
Through whirlpools of joy, on this groovy track.

A Frolic in the Firmament

Up high in the sky, where the clouds do play,
I met a comet having a bad day.
He lost his tail in a twinkling game,
And rolled through the stars, feeling quite lame.

We raced with the moon on a surfboard of light,
As meteors zipped past like they're out of sight.
The sun cracked a joke, and the planets all laughed,
While a nebula giggled, feeling quite daft.

With a bounce and a jig, we danced on a ring,
Where Saturn's got moves that are fit for a king.
A dolphin flipped by, with a twinkle in eye,
"Let's party in space!" he let out a cry.

So we twirled through the cosmos, in laughter and cheer,
Making memories bright, as we spun through the sphere.
In a frolic of joy, our hearts were so light,
We waved to the universe, shining so bright.

The Cosmic Comedians

Two stars in a bar, sipping light-year beer,
Crackin' up jokes, making laughter appear.
A black hole walks in, with a heavy old grin,
"Why did the nebula never lose? 'Cause it spins!"

Galactic stand-up, it's a riot tonight,
With a supernova building a punchline so bright.
"A photon walks in," says the light with a glare,
"And says, 'I'm here for a laugh, if you dare!'"

They jest about comets, tailing in haste,
And how gravity always pulls them to waste.
With every high quip, the moon's rolling on wide,
While asteroids join, adding jokes to the ride.

As laughter erupts across the vast skies,
Even the quasars let out muffled sighs.
In the cosmos of humor, we find such delight,
With cosmic comedians lighting up the night.

Chronological Capers

A chicken crossed time, with a hop and a peep,
To meet a historian, awake from his sleep.
"Why'd you jump timelines?" the old man inquired,
"Too many boring lectures, I felt so retired!"

They traveled to Rome, where a toga-clad gnome,
Said, "Here's where I came from, but it's time to roam!"
With a wink and a nod, they leaped into the past,
Sipping on juice, making memories fast.

Then off to the future, where robots all dance,
Hilarity strikes in a wobbly romance.
"Look at us," they chortled, "we're legends in time,
Making dates error-prone, all while in our rhyme!"

With giggles and gaffes, they sped through the years,
Creating a ruckus, filled with laughter and cheers.
In chronological capers, they found such delight,
Two spirits in motion, shining through the night.

The Dance of Star-Crossed Seconds

In a clock that spins like a top,
Seconds tumble, flip, and hop.
Tick-tock races through the night,
Time waltzes left, it takes the flight.

Planets strut in silly boots,
Dancing round in merry hoots.
Comets join the jiving line,
Shooting stars, they sip on wine.

Galaxies play hide and seek,
Stars peek out, then go antique.
Winks exchanged with playful grace,
Time's a jester in bright space.

Laughing as they swirl and twirl,
In a cosmic dance, they whirl.
With each leap, a giggle shared,
In this universe, none are scared.

Sunlit Galaxies of the Mind

In the bright of thought's delight,
Ideas blast off, taking flight.
Certain musings spin and sway,
As bright ideas play all day.

Nebulas of silly dreams,
Like bubblegum, they burst at seams.
Each notion plays a playful trick,
Like shoots of laughter, quick and slick.

Cosmic giggles, oh what fun,
Thoughts collide like stars unspun.
Every query a jumping star,
Zooming past, so near, yet far.

In a dance of whimsy wide,
Mind's horizons, take a ride.
With every laugh, new worlds unwind,
In sunlit galaxies of the mind.

Looping Through Celestial Jests

Around we go in loops so bright,
Orbiting laughter, pure delight.
Asteroids chuckling on a spree,
They tumble 'round with glee and glee.

A black hole makes a funny face,
Swallowing stars with fluffy grace.
Planets giggle, spin, and twirl,
In the cosmos, thoughts unfurl.

Every comet tells a joke,
With a tail that leaves us woke.
Saturn's rings, they spin and sing,
A cosmic choir in endless spring.

Laughing galaxies collide in zest,
In a dance of humor, they jest.
Round and round, forever we run,
Looping through celestial fun.

Awash in Cosmic Whispers

Whispers drift on stellar breeze,
Tales of mischief float with ease.
Stars exchange their secrets wide,
    Giggles in the inky tide.

Moonbeams tickle sleepy eyes,
  With a wink, they gently rise.
Through the ether, gales of cheer,
  Funny stories, crystal clear.

Supernovae burst with flare,
  Spreading laughter everywhere.
Shooting stars, a comet's grin,
  Laughter echoes from within.

Awash in whispers, soft and bright,
  The universe, a pure delight.
In every twinkle, every gleam,
  Cosmic jesters weave a dream.

The Galactic Gambit

In a ship made of cheese, we zoom through the stars,
Dodging asteroids shaped like old rusty cars.
Alien gamers with green thumbs up,
Challenging us to a cosmic cup.

With dice made of stardust and cards of dark night,
We gamble our hopes in a drifty light flight.
Each roll sends us spiraling, what a wild scene,
Time bends and laughs at our raucous routine.

Hiccups in the Heavens

While floating on clouds, I hiccup a tune,
The cosmos all giggles, an unruly boon.
Stars twinkle with jest as I float upside down,
Gravity's lost in this whimsical town.

A comet zooms past with a corkscrew twirl,
I hiccup again, watch galaxies whirl.
Constellations blush at my silly ballet,
Dancing through time in the quirkiest way.

Celestial Conundrums

Why does Mars wear a tutu, dancing so bright?
And Jupiter's storms throw a wild moonlight.
We're lost in a riddle of comets and laughs,
As time plays its tricks on our parabolic gaffs.

A rogue satellite flings out my lunch,
Cereal floats freely, in the void it does munch.
Each puzzle's a giggle, a twist of the fate,
In a universe laughing, we just can't be late.

Echoes of Entropy

In a vacuum of giggles, where chaos must dwell,
Echoes of laughter ring out like a bell.
Wormholes hiccup, in loops they entwine,
With energy bursts that shimmer and shine.

A T-Rex in space throws a party insane,
With confetti made of quarks, it's all rather plain.
Yet every mistake sends us tumbling round,
In the whirl of confusion, sheer joy can be found.

Time-Looping Larks

In a loop we dance and twirl,
Each moment a quirky swirl,
I spill my drink for the third time,
Yet laugh it off; it's quite sublime.

The clock strikes one, and here we go,
Back to the start, just so you know,
With giggles loud, we try to flee,
But trip on fate quite comically.

Around we spin, a merry chase,
Grinning wide in this funny race,
A déjà vu of wrong turns made,
Oh, sweet loop — we're not dismayed!

So toast again; here's to the fun,
Let's loop till we've both come undone,
In this merry-go-round of the absurd,
We laugh and dance, all sense disturbed.

The Cosmic Circus

Under lights of cosmic glow,
Here titans tumble, stars in tow,
A comet juggles with great flair,
While black holes pull the audience's hair.

Planets pirouette, quite the show,
With rings that dance and twinkle so,
The universe laughs at our fumbles,
As gravity makes us all stumble.

Asteroids bounce with a giggling sound,
While time itself sways round and round,
In this circus, all feel the thrill,
Even light beams take a little spill.

So grab some popcorn, sit right tight,
Enjoy the space-fun, stars so bright,
In this wondrous cosmic parade,
Laughter is the ticket made!

Twists of the Timeless

Around the bend, then back we go,
With goofy grins and winks to show,
A clock that ticks in silly chimes,
Each second spins, defying crimes.

Stretched and squished, reality bends,
Where every misstep easily mends,
With giggles echoing through the void,
A jest of fate we once enjoyed.

In paradox, we joke and tease,
While logic sits beneath the trees,
The universe plays tricks on us,
In laughter loud, it joins the fuss.

So take a leap, and twist away,
In this timeless jest, we'll play,
With every laugh a new surprise,
In the waltz of the cosmic skies.

A Reverie in the Stars

Beneath the stars, a whimsical sight,
We float in dreams, both day and night,
With wishes tossed like comets bright,
And destiny giggles, holding tight.

In starlit talk, the cosmos sings,
Of silly things and wobbly wings,
As moons play tag in vibrant hues,
And nebulae dance with gentle cues.

The Milky Way spills secrets low,
Like candy bars in a cosmic show,
Each twinkle winks, a playful jest,
In this reverie, we feel so blessed.

So let's unfold the galactic fun,
In joy and laughter, we are one,
With dreams so bright, we often chase,
In the starry fields, we find our place.

The Wandering Timebender

A fellow with a twisty clock,
He zips and zooms around the block.
With every tick, he skips a beat,
And leaves behind a trail of feet.

He met a cat from years gone by,
Who leapt through time with a sly pie.
They both just laughed, it was a dance,
A wobbly, giggly, timey prance.

They chatted over cosmic tea,
Swapping stories, wild and free.
A hiccup here, a tumble there,
Chasing echoes everywhere.

In a hiccup, time unwinds,
With bubbles popping, funny finds.
Then off he goes, a wink, a spin,
To dance with time, let the fun begin!

Galactic Games and Mischief

In a field of stars with playful glee,
Aliens gather for a spree.
They toss around some cosmic rocks,
While a space dog barks in his socks.

One green dude just lost his shoe,
Now he hops like a kangaroo.
The laughter echoes, bright and bold,
As stories of their tricks unfold.

A comet flies with style so grand,
Holding ice cream in its hand.
They cheer and shout while racing fast,
In zigzag lines, they laugh at last.

When night falls down, they rest and chat,
Swapping tales of this and that.
Mischief here, a twinkle there,
Galactic friends beyond compare!

Whirling Through Wormholes

Round and round through loops of light,
A chubby astronaut takes flight.
With a belly full of stars to munch,
He swirls on by for an interstellar brunch.

He bumps a squirrel from distant realms,
Who steers a ship with tiny helms.
They giggle as they whip and whirl,
In this strange, absurd, space-time swirl.

Racing past a camp of moons,
They trade their spacey, silly tunes.
A flip, a flop, a laugh or two,
And back they go, who knows where to?

But one wrong turn and oh dear me,
They land where biscuits grow on trees!
With crumbs of joy in every bite,
They feast until the morning light.

The Great Cosmic Caper

Two cosmic pals in a starry ride,
Stole a rocket full of pride.
With winks and grins, they flew so high,
Chasing planets, oh my, oh my!

A bubble bath in a nebula bright,
With rubber ducks, what a sight!
They splashed around, igniting cheers,
While dodging meteors with silly gears.

A tickle fight on a comet's tail,
Giggling loud, they started to sail.
Through gummy asteroids, soft and sweet,
A crunchy snack for their next treat.

With every turn, they spun and twirled,
Creating chaos in a starry world.
At day's end, they headed back,
With a treasure trove of giggles, what a knack!

Enigmas of the Infinite

In a universe so wide and bright,
Planets dance, oh what a sight!
Stars play chess with cosmic glee,
Gravity's just a playful flea.

Galaxies swirl like skirts on a twirl,
Stars shout out, 'Give it a whirl!'
Black holes giggle, 'Watch your back!'
Time's a prankster, never slack.

Comets race in silly sprints,
A moon trips over, "Oops, my prints!"
Asteroids wear hats, think they're cool,
But they tumble like a jesting fool.

Through all this cosmic joke and jest,
We laugh along, it feels the best!
For in this wild, wondrous show,
The punchline's infinite, just so you know!

Rhythm of the Cosmos

In the beat of the universe, things get loud,
Supernovas jump, attracting a crowd.
Stars twinkle disco, with lights on display,
Planets drop it low, in a wild ballet.

Meteor showers rain down with flair,
While black holes spin like they just don't care.
Galactic grooves shake the night so free,
Time's the DJ, mixing history!

Quasars beam with a funky twist,
Lunar craters form a dance floor mist.
Saturn's rings are the bling they flaunt,
Comets slide by with a cosmic taunt.

So come join the maddest interstellar jam,
In the rhythm of the cosmos, be who you am!
Feel the fun as we twist and twold,
In this cosmic dance, we never grow old!

Cosmic Hijinks

There's a star named Benny, quite the joker,
Pulls pranks on comets, oh what a smoker!
"Catch me if you can!" he shouts with a wink,
While planets chuckle, 'Let's not overthink!'

Wormholes are portals, a twisty delight,
Transporting cats in the dead of night.
They land on Mars, strike a pose and pose,
Taking selfies with rocks, feet in a rose!

Meteorites hold a fashion show,
Glittering stones, all aglow.
Neptune gives the thumbs up, feeling grand,
While Jupiter laughs, "Now you're in demand!"

So if you gaze at the skies above,
Remember the laughs, the fun, the love.
For in this vastness, where wonders collide,
Cosmic hijinks play, let joy be your guide!

A Journey through the Fourth Dimension

Jump through time like jumping jacks,
Skip through ages, avoid the cracks.
Past and future laugh as they play,
In the fourth dimension, no dull day.

Meet a dodo with a top hat and cane,
Showing you sights, a glorious train.
Riding on photons, gliding with ease,
Time flies by, like a gentle breeze.

Waves of laughter ripple and flow,
Back to the future, bumbling slow.
"Oops, I'm early!" a time-traveler cries,
While history waves with mischievous eyes.

So pack your bags, and bring some cheer,
A journey through time, the constant sphere.
In this wild ride, join the delight,
As we bounce through dimensions, full of light!

A Starlit Timeline

Bouncing through the cosmic breeze,
Lost in time but feeling free.
Planets spin and stars do twirl,
What a mad and merry whirl!

Cakes of light in orbits bright,
Dance and giggle in the night.
Galaxies play hide and seek,
Wobbling worlds with tiny squeaks.

Wormholes twist with snickers loud,
A cosmic joke for every crowd.
Comets race with silly grace,
Through the universe we chase!

So grab a friend and launch anew,
In this endless cosmic zoo.
With each tick, we laugh and climb,
In the jests of stellar time!

Quasar Quirks

In the blink of a starlit eye,
Quasars wink and giggle by.
Dancing flames of fiery jest,
Make a game of who's the best!

Asteroids in tutus prance,
While black holes spin in cosmic dance.
The pulsars beat a zany tune,
As aliens giggle at the moon.

Galactic gags and playful plots,
Stars collide in one big dot.
Gravity cracks a funny grin,
As light escapes, yet you're still in!

So let's toast with meteor punch,
As we orbit and laugh and crunch.
In this bizarre celestial show,
Who knew the cosmos could be so low?

The Lost Hours

Tick-tock goes the cosmic clock,
Hours lost in time's great shock.
Peeking out from behind the stars,
With a laugh, they've ditched their cars!

Minutes play tag, seconds hide,
In the universe, they take a ride.
Causality trips over its shoes,
As young stars share their silly blues.

The calendar decided to tumble,
Now counts days that jester's jumble.
In parallel realms, we'll meet and greet,
Finding fun in a twisty seat!

So let's drink to the hours we've spun,
In this timeless joke, we've all won.
With laughter echoing far and wide,
In the vastness where giggles collide!

Lightyears of Laughter

Zooming past in a flash so bright,
Laughter echoes through the night.
Traveling far through cosmic glee,
Finding humor in a nebula spree.

Astro-bunnies hop through space,
With a cheeky grin on their face.
They'll tell you that stars are just shy,
Whispering jokes as they fly by.

Rocket ships with disco lights,
Blast off into giggle fights.
Comets sport their silly hats,
As we dance with giggly chats!

In the end, it's all a game,
In this universe, we're all the same.
So let's soar through this zany view,
With lightyears of laughter in our crew!

www.ingramcontent.com/pod-product-compliance
Lightning Source LLC
Chambersburg PA
CBHW051632160426
43209CB00004B/620